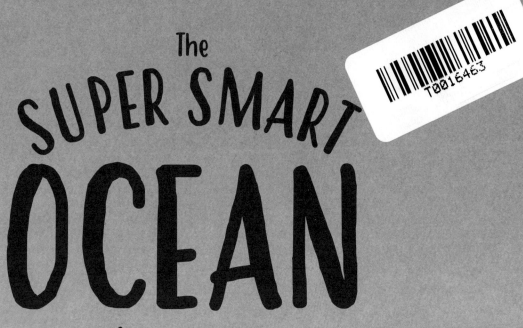

The
SUPER SMART
OCEAN
Activity
Book

By Gemma Barder

Illustrated by
Lucy Zhang

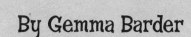

ARCTURUS

ARCTURUS

This edition published in 2023 by Arcturus Publishing Limited
26/27 Bickels Yard, 151–153 Bermondsey Street,
London SE1 3HA

Author: Gemma Barder
Illustrator: Lucy Zhang
Editors: Becca Clunes and Lucy Doncaster
Design: Fountain Creative

ISBN: 978-1-3988-2561-1
CH010450NT
Supplier 29, Date 0123, PI 00000707

Printed in China

What is STEM?

STEM is a world-wide initiative that aims to cultivate
an interest in Science, Technology, Engineering, and
Mathematics, in an effort to promote these disciplines to
as wide a variety of students as possible.

UNDERWATER WONDERS

From whales and walruses to starfish and seahorses, this fact-packed book will take you on an underwater adventure around the world's great oceans. There are more than 65 fabulous puzzles to solve and activities to complete, including spot-the-difference scenes, logic puzzles, mazes, and more!

Did you know?

Although there is technically only one global ocean, scientists today generally recognize five named oceans—the Arctic, Atlantic, Pacific, Indian, and Southern oceans. Together, the water in these oceans covers about 71 percent of Earth's surface!

The Arctic is the coldest ocean, with an average temperature of -2 °C (28 °F). The Indian Ocean is the warmest, with temperatures ranging from 19 °C (66 °F) to a balmy 30 °C (82 °F). The Pacific Ocean is the biggest and deepest—it covers more than twice the surface area of the second largest ocean, the Atlantic!

SLEEPY STINGRAYS

Stingrays are among the most recognizable animals in the ocean.
They move gracefully through the water by "flapping" their fins, but they can
also be potentially dangerous to humans due to the sting in their long, thin tails.
Circle every other letter to find out where stingrays like to take a nap.
The first letter has been circled for you.

(u) c n v d r e t r h t j h v e b s a a s n m d p

u

Stingrays are carnivorous,
which means they only eat
meat. They live off worms,
crustaceans, and fish.

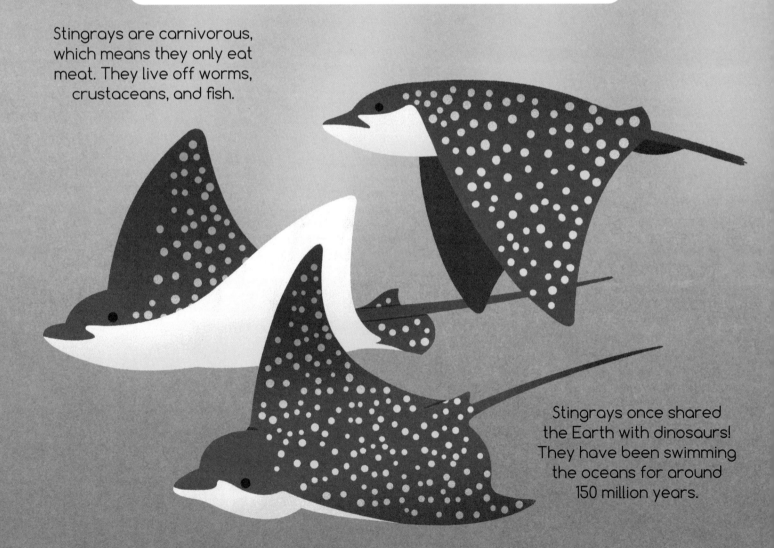

Stingrays once shared
the Earth with dinosaurs!
They have been swimming
the oceans for around
150 million years.

CORAL SEARCH

The Great Barrier Reef in Australia's Coral Sea is full of amazing animals and beautiful coral. Can you find the following coral sequences in the grid?

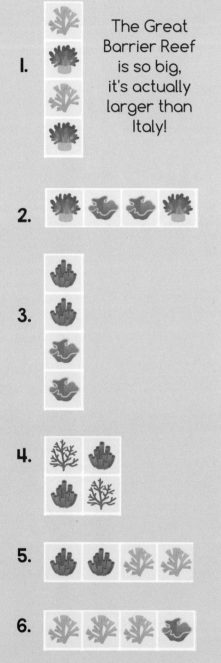

The Great Barrier Reef is so big, it's actually larger than Italy!

It is home to some of the world's most dangerous underwater animals, including the box jellyfish.

NOW YOU SEE HIM, NOW YOU DON'T!

The mimic octopus uses clever camouflaging techniques to hide itself from predators. Circle the octopuses you can see here.

Even though it is not poisonous, the mimic octopus knows just how to look like a poisonous animal, to warn away predators.

As well as changing hue, the mimic octopus twists its body into different shapes to make it look like other animals!

SNAZZY SEA SNAIL

Sea snails have been found across the world's oceans, from close to shore to the deepest trench, and from tropical seas to the Antarctic! Finish off this sea snail using a fancy design.

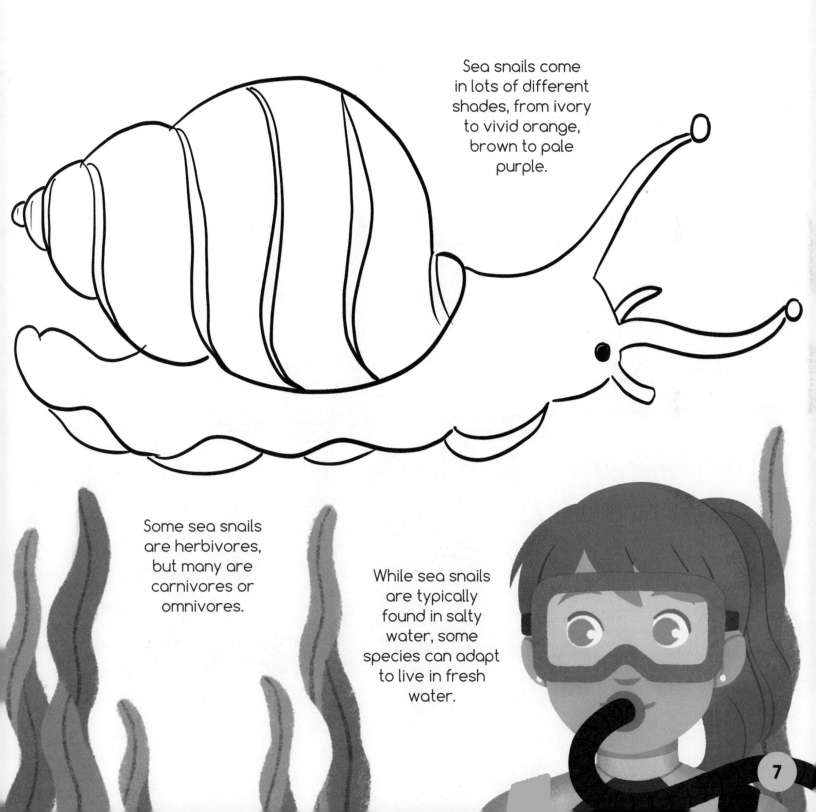

Sea snails come in lots of different shades, from ivory to vivid orange, brown to pale purple.

Some sea snails are herbivores, but many are carnivores or omnivores.

While sea snails are typically found in salty water, some species can adapt to live in fresh water.

CLOWNING AROUND

You might think these clownfish are identical, but there are actually four matching pairs to be found. Can you match them up?

Clownfish use clicking and popping noises to let other clownfish know who's boss.

Clownfish dance with anemones before they make their homes inside them.

STARFISH SUDOKU

Starfish are incredible animals (they aren't fish!). Read these amazing facts, then complete the grid below. There should be one of each type of starfish in each column, row, and mini-grid.

Starfish have a tough layer of skin to protect them from predators. Some species even have spikes as added protection.

Their eyes are on the ends of their arms!

A starfish can grow a new arm if one is damaged by a predator!

Cushion starfish

Blue sea star

Common starfish

Fromia starfish

SEA CAVE SPOTTING

Sea caves are formed as seawater slowly washes away the rock from a cliff over hundreds of millions of years! Can you spot and circle eight differences between these two images?

The world's biggest sea cave can
be found on the Otago coast of
New Zealand. The Matainaka cave
is 1.5 km (just under a mile) long.

TRENCH TRUTHS

The Mariana Trench in the western Pacific Ocean is the deepest ocean trench in the world. It is full of mysteries yet to be uncovered. Read each fact below and check the box for true or false. Turn to page 87 to find out if you were right!

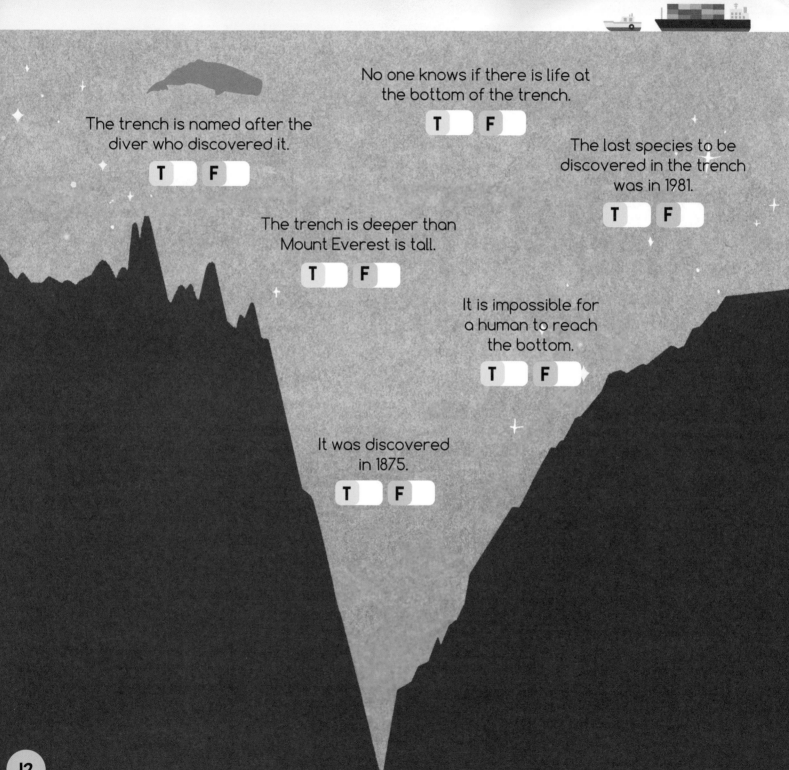

No one knows if there is life at the bottom of the trench.

T F

The trench is named after the diver who discovered it.

T F

The last species to be discovered in the trench was in 1981.

T F

The trench is deeper than Mount Everest is tall.

T F

It is impossible for a human to reach the bottom.

T F

It was discovered in 1875.

T F

DINNER TIME!

The food chain is vital to marine creatures' survival. Sea plants are eaten by tiny animals, which are eaten by larger ones, and so on up the food chain to the top carnivores. Follow the lines to find out what these ocean animals like to feast on.

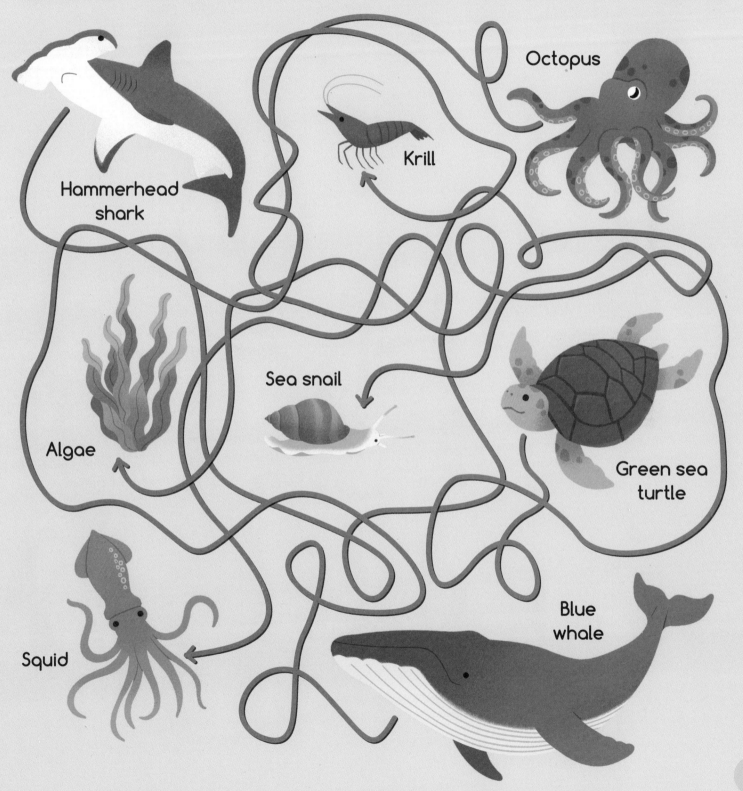

SEAWEED TANGLE

Seaweed provides a safe haven for all kinds of sealife. Can you find your way through this seaweed maze? How many fish do you pass?

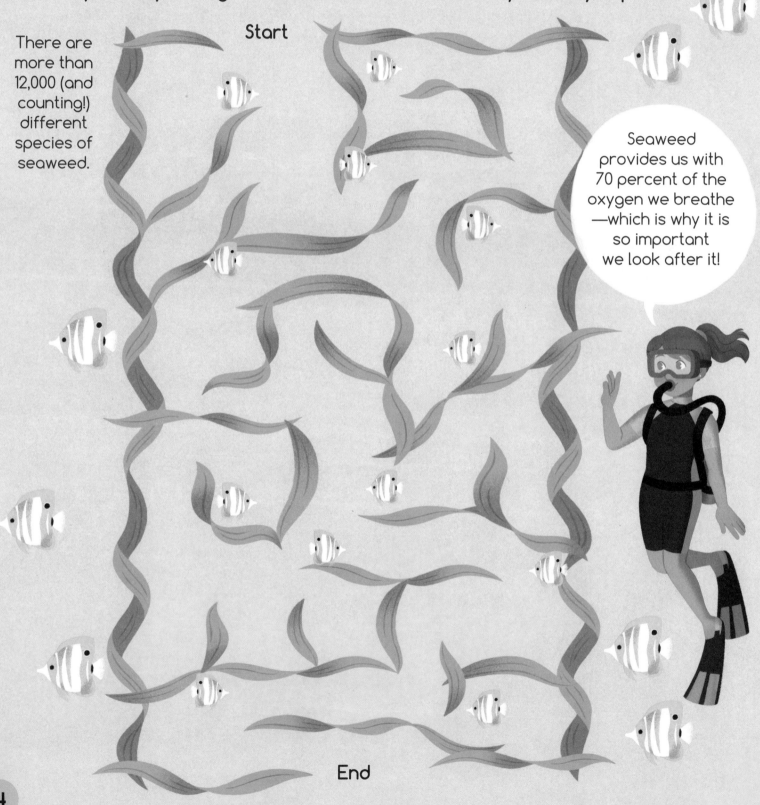

There are more than 12,000 (and counting!) different species of seaweed.

Start

Seaweed provides us with 70 percent of the oxygen we breathe —which is why it is so important we look after it!

End

DOLPHIN DILEMMA

Dolphins are some of the ocean's most intelligent animals. Take a look at the picture below and see if you can find the correct missing pieces.

Dolphins are great at chatting to each other. They use body language, squeaks, and whistles to tell each other the news.

They mostly eat fish, squid, jellyfish, shrimp, and octopuses.

A

B

C

D

E

F

DOWN IN THE DEEP

The bottom of the ocean is a mysterious place, with lots of animals yet to be discovered. Take a look at the image below and see how many of each listed item you can find. Write the number in the box.

Anglerfish

Viperfish

Rattails

Football fish

Blue tangs

A female rattail fish can release as many as 100,000 eggs.

Viperfish live so deep in the ocean that they are rarely seen by humans.

The football fish is a type of anglerfish. It was given its name by a zoologist in 1833. Female football fish are larger than male ones.

WONDERFUL WALRUS

Can you complete this fact file using answers from the list?

Tusks

16 km (10 miles)

100 cm (40 in)

2 tonnes (2.2 tons)

40 years

How long does the average walrus live?

How far away can a walrus' song be heard?

How long is the average walrus' tusk?

Which part of its body does a walrus use to hunt and to pull itself out of the water?

How much can a male walrus weigh?

PEARL PERFECTION

Pearls are formed when a speck of sand or grit gets into certain types of oyster, mussel, or clam shells. The mollusk reacts by coating the speck in layers of special fluid, which build up to make a pearl. Work out how many pearls to draw in each shell by solving these puzzles.

The Pearl of Puerto is the biggest pearl ever found. It is 67 cm (26.3 in) wide. That's about the same width as a soccer ball!

1. You have baked a cake to share with three friends. You cut it equally and give each friend a slice. How many slices have you cut?

2. What is 100 divided by 20?

3. How many prongs are there on a trident?

4. How many eyes does an animal with binocular vision have?

SILHOUETTE MATCH

Can you find the silhouette that matches this seahorse exactly?

The top of a seahorse's head (sometimes called the crown) is as unique as a fingerprint.

A

B

C

D

E

Seahorses love company and like swimming in pairs with their tails hooked together.

DOTTY SWIMMER

Starting at 1, complete this picture to work out what creature this is!

These animals have been on Earth for around 110 million years!

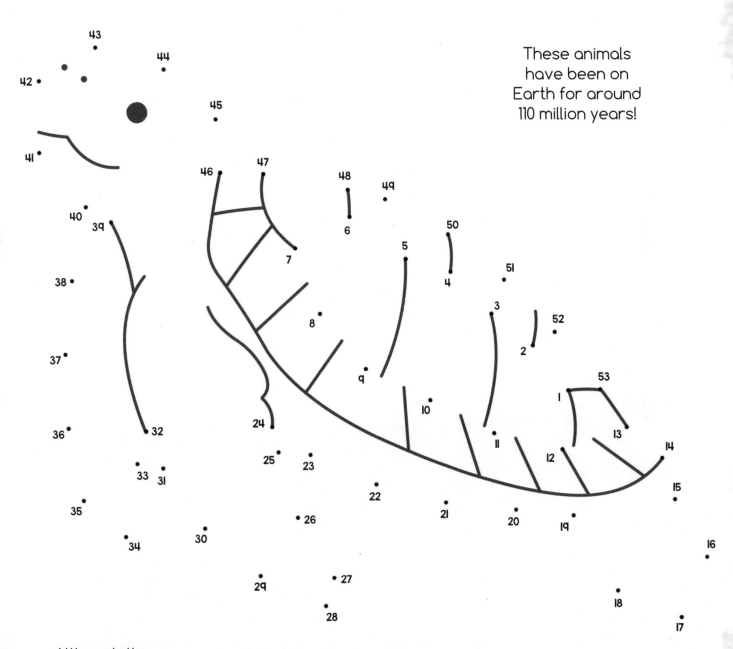

Although they breathe air, they can stay under water for hours at a time.

UNDERWATER CODE

Use the code cracker to discover what each of these whales is called.

A	B	C	D	E	F	G	H	I	J	K	L	M	N	O	P
$	*	&	/	£	?	☺	@	§	«	🍎	♡	+	»	ʒ	=

Q	R	S	T	U	V	W	X	Y	Z	<	?	_	"	!	~
†	#	∞	‡	✈	•	€	‹	›	¢	¥	∞	©	°	®	↕

*♡✈£
€@$♡£

*£♡✈☺$
€@$♡£

∞=£#+
€@$♡£

@✈+=*$&🍎
€@$♡£

There are two types of whale—baleen, which have filters instead of teeth, and toothed whales. Baleen whales eat masses of tiny sea animals, while toothed ones eat larger prey.

22

PICKY EATERS

Herbivores are animals that eat plants, carnivores eat meat, and omnivores like both! Can you sort these animals into these categories? Draw a circle next to the herbivores, a square next to the carnivores, and a triangle for the omnivores.

Tuna

Angelfish

Bonnethead shark

Green sea turtle

Orca

Walrus

Porpoise

Great white shark

Saltwater crab

ANGLER ART

Anglerfish use a special light to lure their prey close enough to catch.
Use the grid below to copy the anglerfish into the grid, opposite.

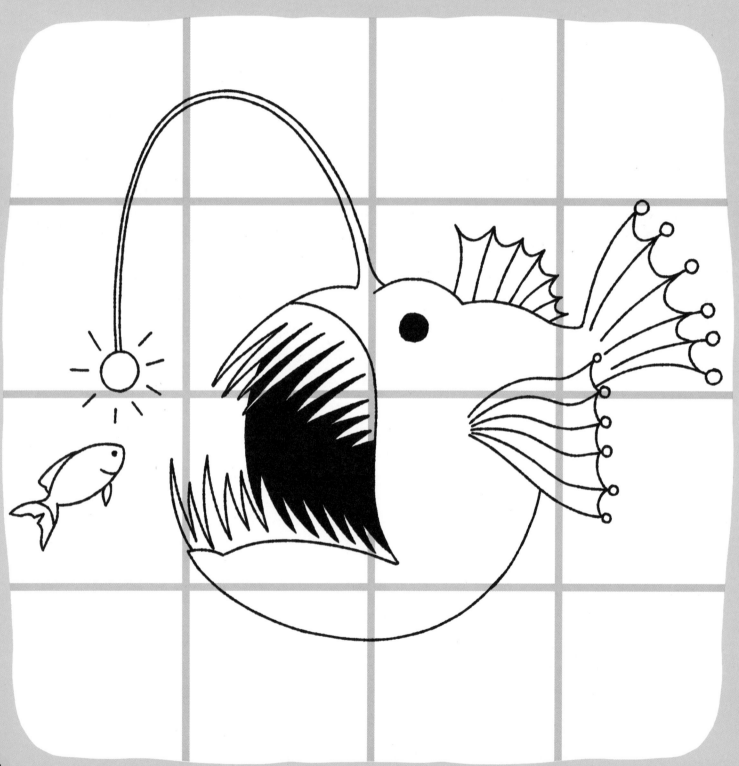

Anglerfish usually just drift through the water, waiting for prey to come to them. However, they can swim really fast if they think they are in danger!

UNDERWATER ERUPTIONS

Did you know that there are volcanoes in the ocean? From time to time they erupt, sometimes causing huge tidal waves. Quickly make your way through this maze from top to bottom before the volcanoes erupt again!

Start

The largest underwater volcano is 273 km (170 miles) long and is called Pūhāhonu, which is Hawaiian for "turtle surfacing for air."

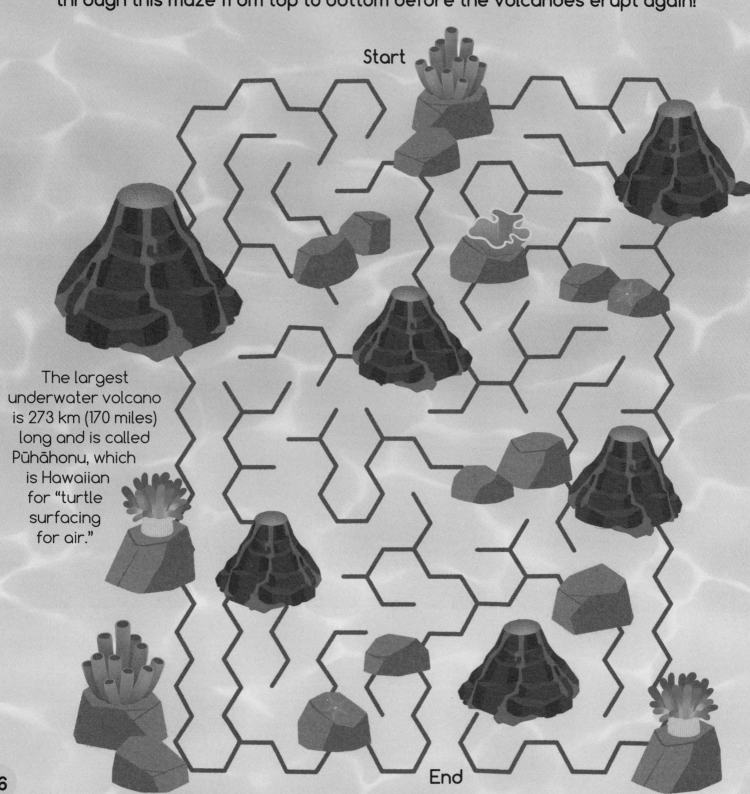

End

SMALL SWIMMERS

Oceans contain some of the world's biggest animals, but they are home to some tiny ones, too! Complete this grid using images of these teeny fish just once in each column, row, and mini-grid.

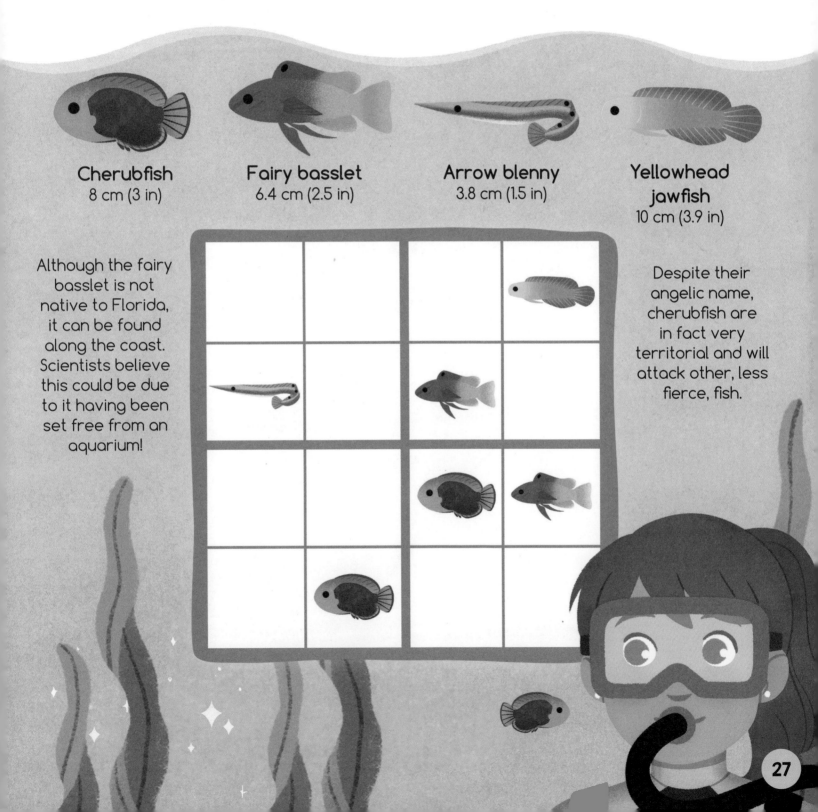

Cherubfish
8 cm (3 in)

Fairy basslet
6.4 cm (2.5 in)

Arrow blenny
3.8 cm (1.5 in)

Yellowhead jawfish
10 cm (3.9 in)

Although the fairy basslet is not native to Florida, it can be found along the coast. Scientists believe this could be due to it having been set free from an aquarium!

Despite their angelic name, cherubfish are in fact very territorial and will attack other, less fierce, fish.

FLAT FLYERS

Take a look at this incredible reef scene, where stingrays swim alongside other flatfish.
Can you spot and circle the following items?

 8 shells

 10 starfish

 6 sea snails

Each stingray has a venomous sting in its tail, although most are not dangerous to humans.

Stingrays move through the water in two ways: Some species use their whole bodies to make waves and others flap their fins like underwater birds!

Stingrays can live for up to 25 years.

Their flat shape makes it easier for them to hide from predators on the sea floor.

CRYSTAL CLEAR

These crystal jellyfish can be found off the coast of North America.
Although they are virtually see-through, they have tiny, light-producing
organs that glow when they are shocked or feeling under threat. Can
you finish drawing the long tentacles on each jellyfish?

A crystal jellyfish's
tentacles are very
poisonous and
could be deadly
to humans.

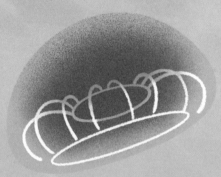

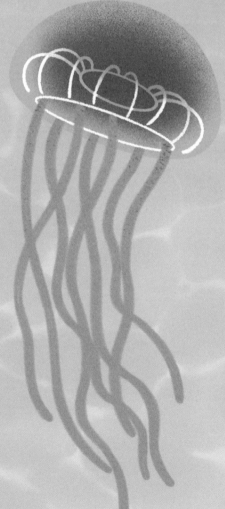

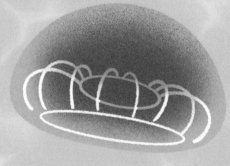

THE GREATEST SHARK!

Great white sharks have a bit of a scary reputation, but they are amazing animals! Read each fact below and check the box for true or false. Turn to page 90 to find out if you were right!

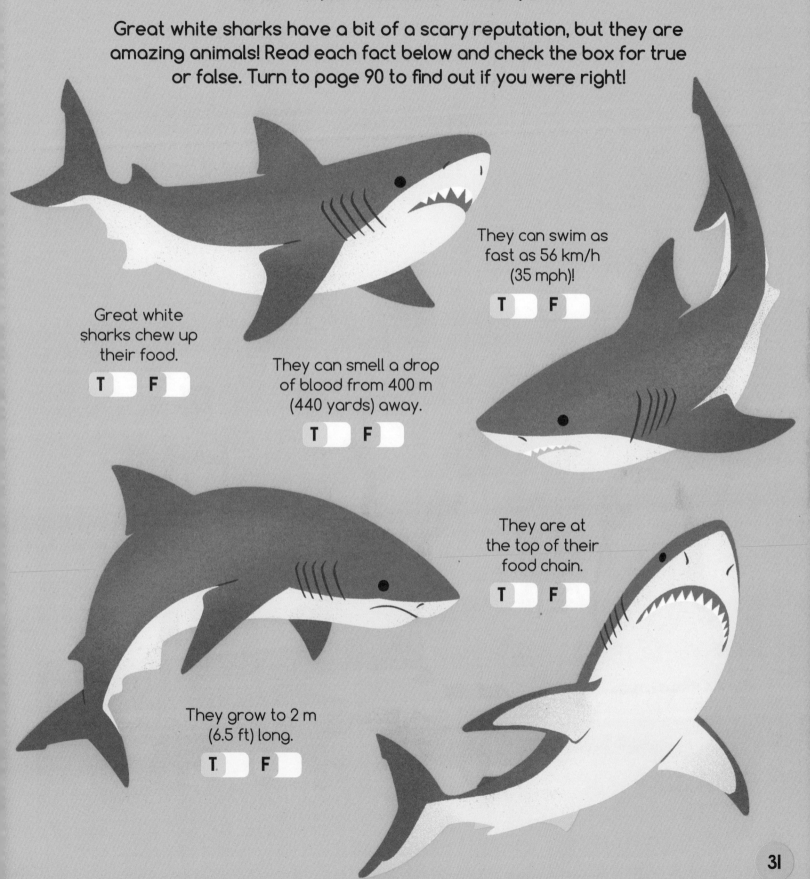

They can swim as fast as 56 km/h (35 mph)!

T ▢ F ▢

Great white sharks chew up their food.

T ▢ F ▢

They can smell a drop of blood from 400 m (440 yards) away.

T ▢ F ▢

They are at the top of their food chain.

T ▢ F ▢

They grow to 2 m (6.5 ft) long.

T ▢ F ▢

PENGUIN PICK

Some types of penguin make their home on the frozen land of Antarctica. Take a look at these two pictures and see if you can spot eight differences between them.

A penguin chick stays with its parents for several months, until it has developed waterproof feathers and can look after itself.

FISH SUPPER

These seabirds could not survive without the ocean to provide them with food! Follow the lines to find out which one has its eye on the fish.

Puffin

Black guillemot

Gannet

CRAB COLLECTION

Crabs come in all different shapes and sizes. Take a look at the line-ups below to see if you can work out which crab should come next.

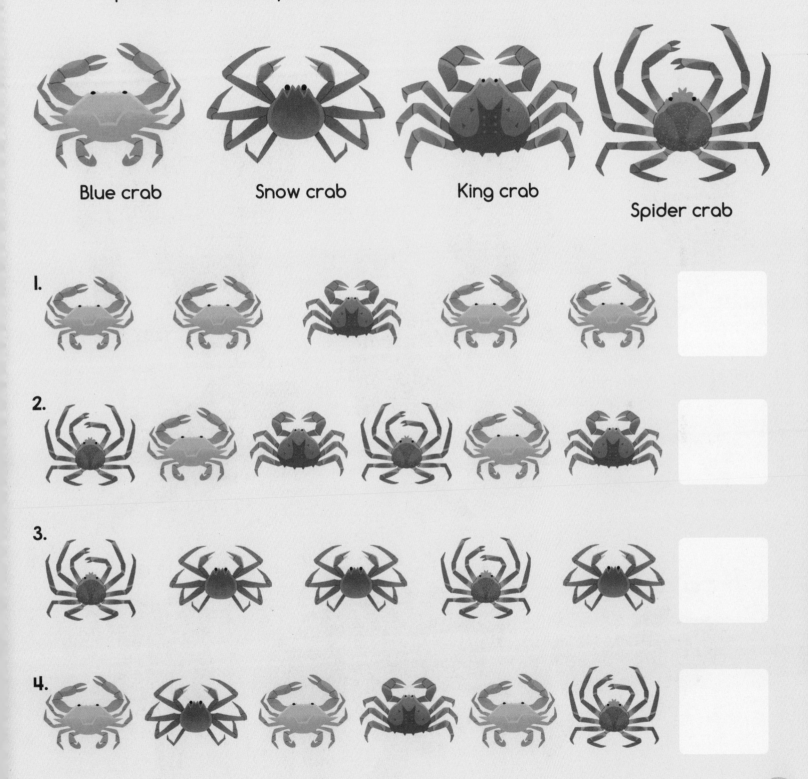

Blue crab   Snow crab   King crab   Spider crab

1.

2.

3.

4.

OTTERLY ADORABLE

Did you know sea otters hold hands to stop them drifting apart when they are asleep? See if you can find four sets of matching pictures—the otters may be on their own or in pairs.

Sea otters have the thickest fur of any animal. This helps them to keep warm, so they always take good care of it by grooming themselves everyday.

Can you draw a friend for this otter, then shade in the picture?

UNDER THE SEA

The reason we know so much about the sea is down to explorers and marine biologists who study life in the ocean. Take a look at this picture of divers exploring, then see if you can find the missing pieces.

Flippers make swimming easier, and masks allow divers to see underwater.

Humans are able to explore the underwater world thanks to special diving equipment. A diver breathes oxygen from a tank carried on the back using a special tube that goes into the mouth.

A

C

E

B

D

F

HORSES AND DRAGONS

Seahorses and seadragons are some of the most unusual animals in the sea. Use the alphabet code to work out the names of the animals below!

a	b	c	d	e	f	g	h	i	j	k	l	m	n	o	p
Code: z	e	q	w	v	u	t	s	c	p	h	o	n	m	l	k

q	r	s	t	u	v	w	x	y	z	<	?	-	"	!	~
Code: a	i	r	g	x	y	d	f	b	j	!	@	#	^	*	&

Some seadragons can reach up to 45 cm (18 in) in length

gslimb
rvzslirv

dvvwb
rvzwiztlm

ovzub
rvzwiztlm

kbtnb
rvzslirv

TERRIFIC TUNA!

Match the answers to the facts to discover the truth about tuna! Then see if you can spot which one of the fish in the bottom picture matches the top one.

How many Atlantic bluefin tuna can be found in a school?

How fast can yellowfin tuna swim?

How long can the Atlantic bluefin tuna grow?

How heavy was the biggest tuna ever caught?

How deep can a southern bluefin tuna dive in a day?

45

678 kg (1,496 lb)

1,000 m (3,280 ft)

74 km/h (46 mph)

3 m (10 ft)

CRUSTACEAN CONUNDRUM

Each of these lobsters and crabs has a matching pair,
apart from one. Can you find the odd one out?

SLIP-SLIDING SEA LIONS

Work out the answers to the equations, then look along the grid.
Which sea lion should you circle?

* Start at A1
* Move north (12 ÷ 3)
* Move east (110 – 105)
* Move south (41 – 40)
* Move west (33 ÷ 11)
* Move north (28 – 22)
* Move east (96 ÷ 12)

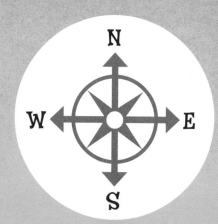

Sea lions are often confused with seals, but there are big differences! Sea lions can walk and run on their flippers, plus they have little flaps over their ears.

Sea lions are super speedy in the water. They have a top swimming speed of about 40 km/h (25 mph).

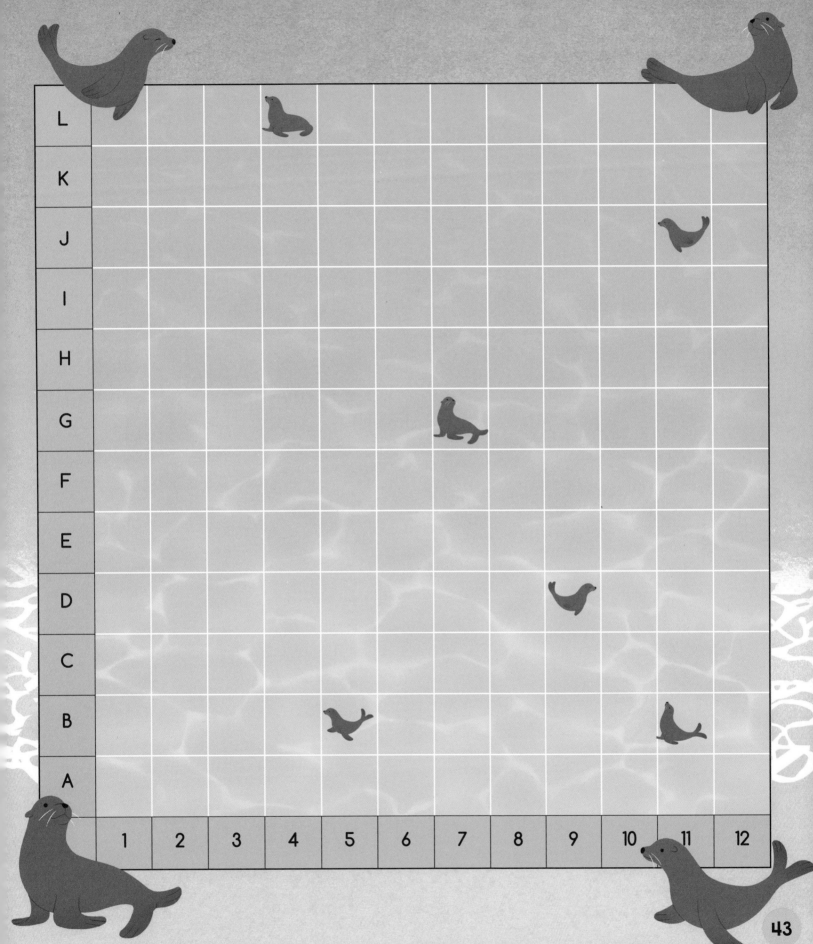

POOL PUZZLER

Rock pools are formed when the tide goes out, leaving seawater in small rock formations. Each of these rock-pool dwellers represents a number. Can you work out which number is represented by each animal?

$5 + $  $ = 11$

Sea sticklebacks are unusual because they do not have scales. Instead, some species have bony plates.

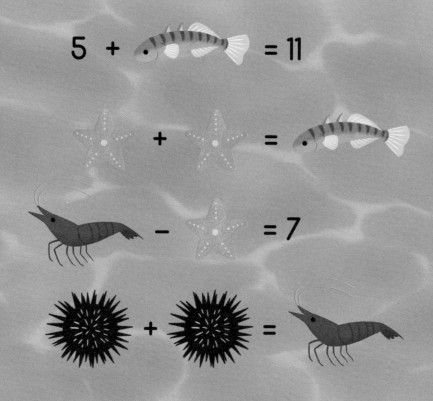

Sea urchins move about on tube-like feet, which move in and out of their shells very quickly, propelling the sea urchins along.

Sea urchin

Starfish

Sea stickleback

Shrimp

TROPICAL TRIP-UP

Tropical oceans are home to all kinds of bright fish.
Can you put this image back in the correct order?

The tropical fish in this picture are a Moorish idol (top left), a daisy parrotfish (bottom left), and a damselfish (right).

Despite looking pretty, damselfish can be aggressive!

A   B   C   D   E   F

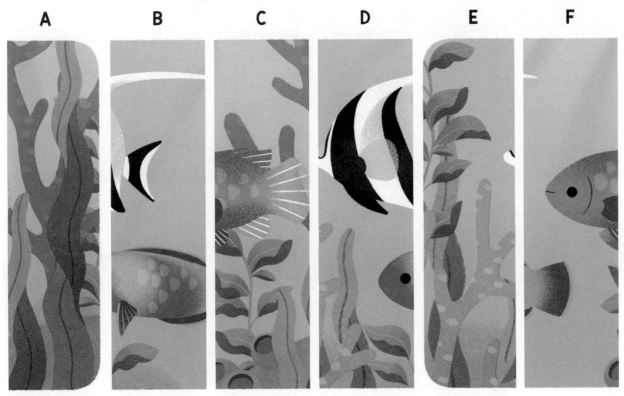

The daisy parrotfish is also known as the bullethead parrotfish because of the shape of its head!

The pattern on the Moorish idol is unique to each fish, like a fingerprint.

SAFE HAVEN

Although they may look like plants, sea anemones are actually animals!
What's more, they sting their prey. Clownfish have a protective coat that means
they can live inside anemones. Which missing pieces belong in this picture?

A

B

C

D

E

F

PLASTIC PROBLEM

Ecosystems in the ocean are under threat from littering and pollution. Take a look at this picture and see if you can spot and circle all the plastic bottles.

A plastic bottle can last for up to 450 years in the ocean. It breaks down into small bits, which sea animals eat. This harms them.

Turn to page 86 to see how you can help clean up the oceans for real!

DOT TO DOT

Follow the dots to draw this image of a well-known sea creature!
Can you work out what it is?

These animals like to hide away under rocks during the day, then come out at night to find food.

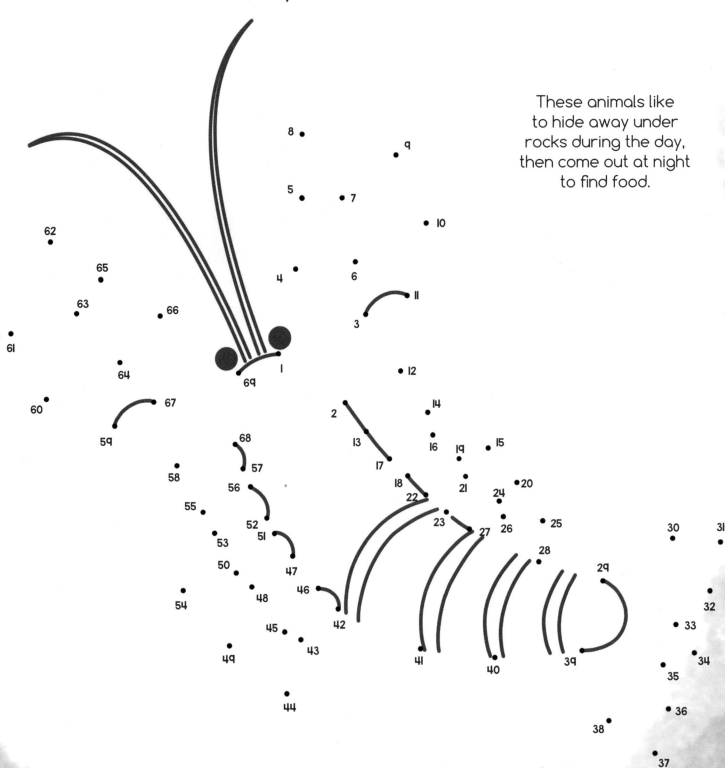

PICK A PEN!

Sea pens are some of the strangest creatures in the ocean. Take a look at the ones below to see if you can spot the odd one out!

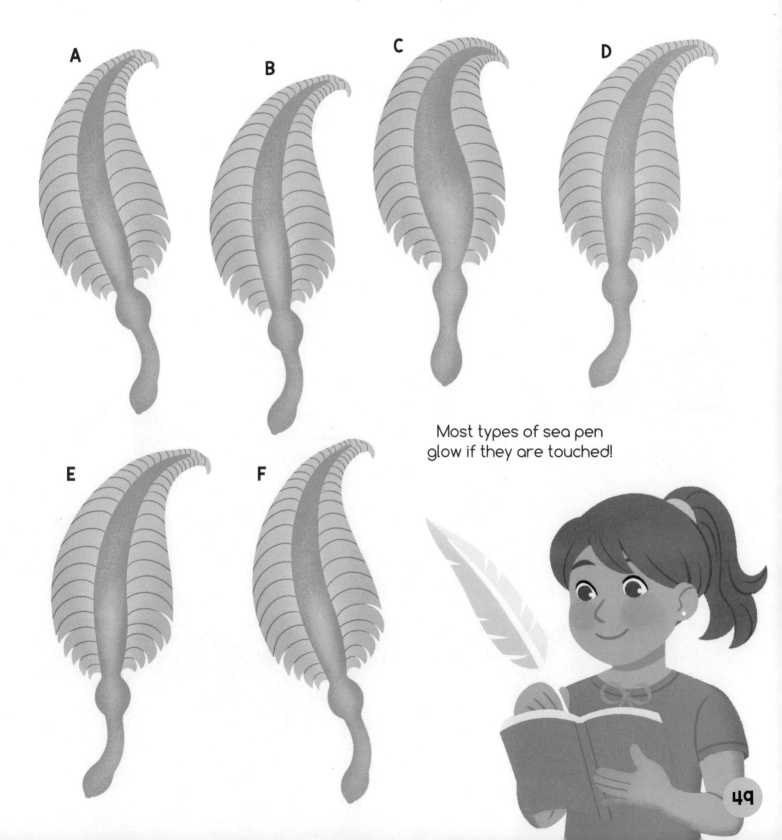

A

B

C

D

Most types of sea pen glow if they are touched!

E

F

THE GREAT BARRIER REEF

The Great Barrier Reef in Australia is the world's largest coral reef. Take a look at the image below to see if you can find and tick off the items on the list.

The Great Barrier Reef can be seen all the way from the surface of the Moon!

Humans also like to visit reefs, to wonder at the creatures that live there.

Coral provides a vibrant home for all sorts of sea creatures, from shrimp and sponges to starfish and squid!

SKATE TO VICTORY!

Sea skaters glide along the surface of the ocean, living off algae that float to the top. Can you work out which skater started skating at 1, 2, and 3?

IDENTICAL ISLAND

Islands come in all different shapes and sizes, and are home to lots of animals.
Take a look at this one. Which of the images below is its true reflection?

Small islands such as this one are sometimes called islets, cays, or keys. A group of small islands is called an archipelago.

Hint: Place a mirror upright along the flat parts of the islands.

KELP CONUNDRUM

Sea kelp are large algae—a vital part of the ocean's ecosystem.
Can you find the matching pairs below? Circle the kelp with no matching pair.

When there is a lot of kelp in one place, it is called a kelp forest.

STINGRAY RIDDLE!

Three pieces of this stingray picture are missing.
Can you find the right ones to make the picture whole again?

Stingrays have no bones in their body, which makes them super-flexible!

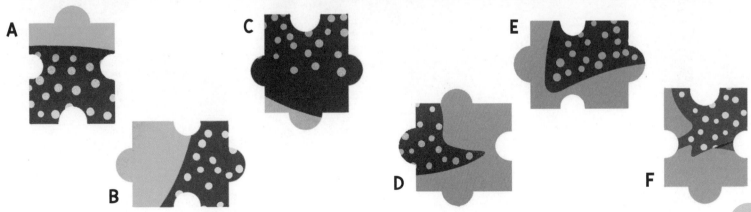

A

B

C

D

E

F

PORPOISE PUZZLE

Read the questions to reveal which of these porpoises is being described:

* It does not have black on it.
* It is not the smallest.
* It has a dorsal fin.

Vaquita

Burmeister's porpoise

Spectacled porpoise

Although they look similar, a dolphin is not a porpoise. A dolphin has a longer nose and its dorsal (top) fin is more curved.

Narrow-ridged finless porpoise

Dall's porpoise

Indo-Pacific finless porpoise

SEASHELL SEQUENCE

Seashells come in lots of different shapes, sizes, and shades.
Each of these pretty shells represents a number. Can you work
out which number is represented by each shell?

Animals build their shells from a mineral called calcium carbonate, which they get from the ocean environment.

Seashells, especially cowrie shells, were once used as currency in China and India.

Scallop shell

Cowrie shell

Nautilus shell

Sand dollar shell

ECHO LOCATION

A sperm whale uses echolocation to determine the position of things in the sea, by making a sound and listening to the noise that is echoed back from objects. Can you work out the answer to each of the equations and then draw the animal on the correct distance, as shown by the vertical lines.

Sperm whales have the largest brain of any animal on Earth! They also make the loudest sound of any animal.

They can dive really, really deep! They have been recorded going down as far as 2,000 m (6,562 ft). It's a good job they can hold their breath for up to about 90 minutes!

1   2   3   4   5

9 + 5 =   12 ÷ 3 =

6   7   8   9   10   11   12   13   14   15

10 ÷ 2 = ☐   1 + 7 = ☐   15 – 4 = ☐   3 × 3 = ☐

WHIP SMARTS

Take a look at this underwater scene. Can you work out which clump of red sea whip is the odd one out?

Although it looks like a plant, red sea whip is an animal that feeds on plankton.

WALRUS SEPARATION

Can you divide these walruses by drawing two further straight lines on the picture? Each walrus should be in its own section of ice.

A male Pacific walrus can grow to up to 3.6 m (12 ft) long!

PLANKTON PILE-UP

Although plankton are tiny, they are very important to the ocean ecosystem. How many of these tiny animals can you spot below?

Plankton are tiny living things that drift in water. They can be plants, animals, bacteria, or fungi.

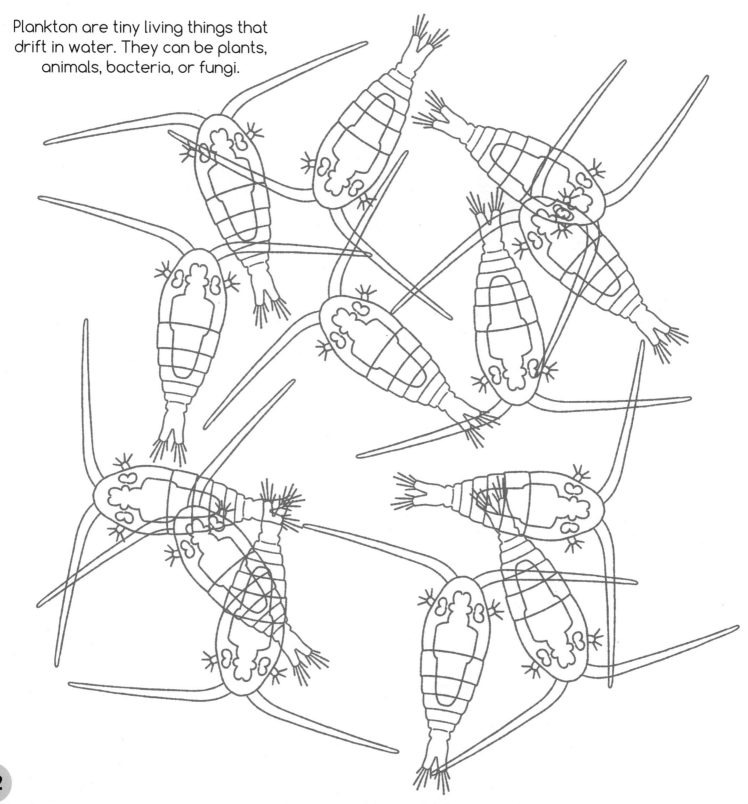

SPECTACULAR LIONFISH

Read the amazing facts about lionfish below, then turn the page
and see if you can answer all the questions.

Female lionfish can
each produce 2 million
eggs a year!

Lionfish are
carnivores and eat
over 50 different
types of fish.

They have venom in the
spines along their backs
to protect them against
predators.

They are mostly
nocturnal (which means
they are awake during
the night!).

SPECTACULAR LIONFISH

Draw in the lionfish's impressive fins here
and answer the questions below!

I. When are lionfish awake?

2. Which part of a lionfish's body contains venom?

3. How many types of fish do they eat?

4. How many eggs do they each produce a year?

SQUID QUIZ

Giant squid live deep in the ocean, which means they are a bit of a mystery to marine biologists. Read each fact below and check the box for true or false. Turn to page 94 to find out if you were right!

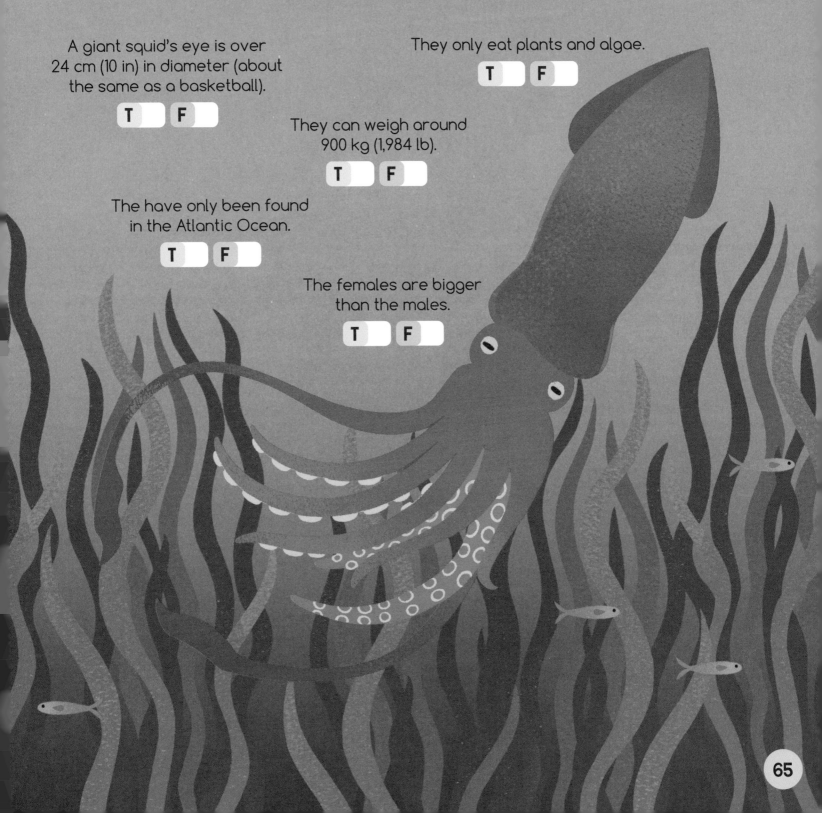

A giant squid's eye is over 24 cm (10 in) in diameter (about the same as a basketball).

T   F

They only eat plants and algae.

T   F

They can weigh around 900 kg (1,984 lb).

T   F

The have only been found in the Atlantic Ocean.

T   F

The females are bigger than the males.

T   F

SUBAQUATIC STINGERS

Some underwater animals are venomous, while others are not, even if they look fierce. Circle the ones below that are marked with a prime number—these are the ones to watch out for!

18
Horseshoe crab

7
Box jellyfish

53
Blue-ringed octopus

25
Dugong

Not all venomous animals are harmful to humans, but unless you know for sure, it is always safer to keep your distance.

13
Marbled cone snail

27
Tiger shark

SELFIE TIME!

Take a good look at the underwater images these divers have taken, below, then turn the page to see how much you remember!

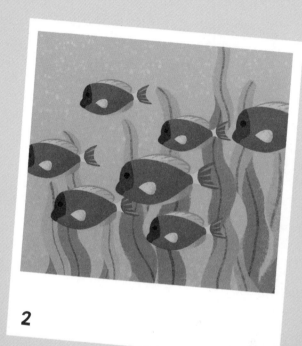

1

2

3

4

SELFIE TIME!

1. How many fish (blue hippo tangs) are in picture 2?

2. Were the divers wearing goggles in picture 4?

3. Did you see any yellow coral in any of the pictures?

4. What animal is behind the diver in picture 1?

5. Which picture showed orange fish?

6. How many fingers is the diver holding up in picture 4?

Divers can usually go down to a limit of 40 m (130 ft). The deepest point in the ocean is 10,935 m (35,876 ft)!

The record time a freediver has held their breath for is 24 minutes and 37 seconds, in 2021. The marine mammal record is 137 minutes! It was set by a Cuvier's beaked whale in 2014.

JELLYFISH LINE-UP

Using just four straight lines, can you connect each of these white-spotted jellyfish without taking your pencil off the page and without going through any jellyfish more than once? It doesn't matter if the line extends to the side, below, or above the jellyfish on the outside of the pattern. We've done the first line for you.

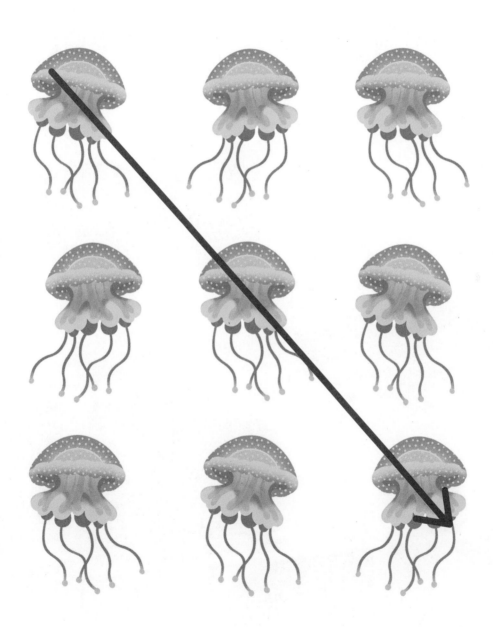

STRENGTH IN NUMBERS

Work out the answers to these number puzzles, then draw lines to match them up with that number of elephant seals.

30 – 25 =

36 ÷ 6 =

Elephant seals are the second largest type of seal in the world. Adult males weigh as much as 3,990 kg (8,800 lb)!

15 ÷ 5 =

0.5 + 0.5 =

48 ÷ 12 =

CODE NAMES

Use the the code below to discover the names of these sharks!

	A	B	C	D	E	F	G	H	I	J	K	L	M	N	O	P
Code:	%	?	*	€	1	§	$	6	9	/	@	!	2	·	3	†

	Q	R	S	T	U	V	W	X	Y	Z	‹	?	_	"	!	~
Code:	Δ	£	8	#	5	«	¶	0	‡	7	‡	¥	4	¢	↕	©	=

2 1 $ % 2 3 5 # 6
8 6 % £ @

! 1 2 3 •
8 6 % £ @

• 5 £ 8 1
8 6 % £ @

* 3 3 @ 9 1 * 5 # # 1 £
8 6 % £ @

There are over 500 different shark species, found in nearly every marine habitat.

71

SHIPWRECK RUMMAGE

The ocean isn't just home to amazing animals, there are also the remains of long-lost ships. Take a look at the image below and see how many of each listed item you can find. Write the number in the box.

Starfish

Lobsters

Pink coral

Blue tangs

Anchors

There are an estimated 3 million shipwrecks on ocean floors around the world!

Shipwrecks provide homes and places to hide for all sorts of sea animals.

73

DOLPHIN DEEP DIVE

Can you draw lines between these dolphins and their names?
Read the clues to help you!

Dusky dolphin
It has the shortest nose.

Ocean dolphins belong
to a group called
Delphinidae. There are
over 30 species within
this group.

Bottlenose dolphin
It is smooth and sleek.

Spinner dolphin
It has a long, pointed nose.

Atlantic spotted dolphin
It lives up to its name!

FOSSIL FINDERS

Fossils of ancient marine animals tell us a lot about life in the oceans millions of years ago. Can you fill in the correct letters to link each fossil to the silhouettes in the box?

Ammonites were sea animals that lived inside a spiral shell. They are related to the octopuses and squid we still have in our oceans today!

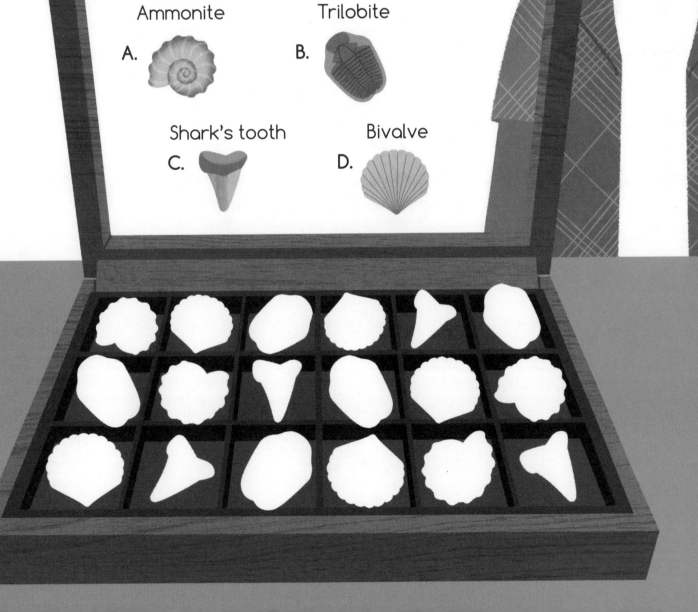

Ammonite

A.

Trilobite

B.

Shark's tooth

C.

Bivalve

D.

DEEP SEA MISSION

Follow the directions to find out where the submarine is heading.

* Start at A1
* North 2
* East 7
* North 3
* West 2
* South 3
* West 1
* North 4
* West 3

Scientists use submarines to study and explore the depths of the ocean and the life in it.

POWER OF EIGHT

Which of these giant octopuses is the odd one out?

Octopuses are super brainy and have excellent memories!

TURTLE TRAIL

Sea turtles emerge out of the ocean when they are ready lay their eggs.
Follow the sequence to get from the sea to the beach. You can move up,
down, left, and right, but not diagonally.

Start here

Follow this sequence

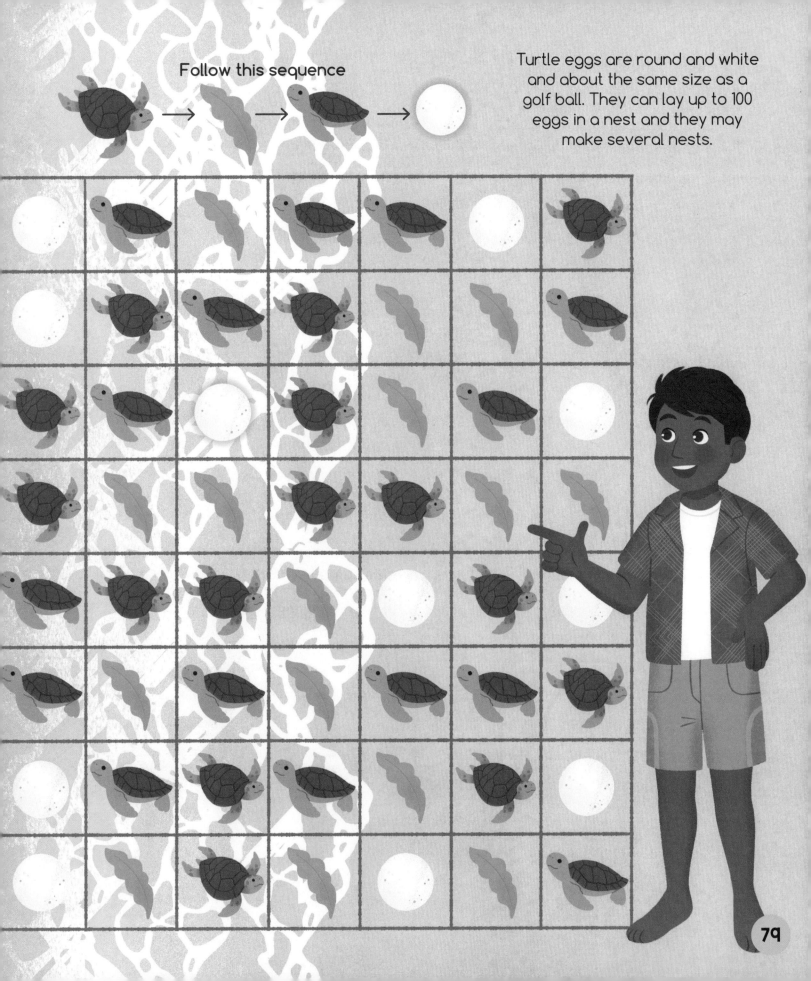

Turtle eggs are round and white and about the same size as a golf ball. They can lay up to 100 eggs in a nest and they may make several nests.

79

PENGUIN FACTS!

Can you match these facts to the penguin they belong to?

These penguins prefer a warmer place to nest and have white markings around their eyes.

King penguin

These don't slide on their bellies like most penguins. Instead, they prefer to hop about on land.

Australia little penguin

These penguins have orange and black beaks. Their chicks have large, shaggy feathers that make them look bigger than their parents!

Galápagos penguin

This type is sometimes called the "fairy penguin" because of its small size!

Rockhopper penguin

SEAHORSE SORT

Seahorses are a type of fish! Unlike most other animals, the male is the one to carry the babies, once the female has laid her eggs in a special pouch. Can you count how many of each type is in this jumble, then write the number in the box?

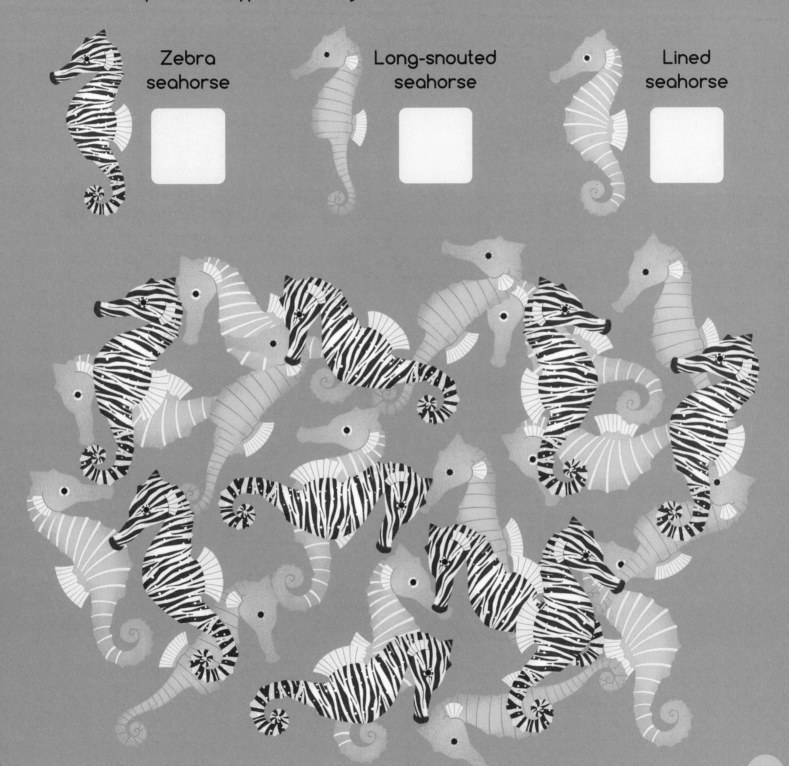

Zebra seahorse

Long-snouted seahorse

Lined seahorse

BEAUTIFUL BETTAS

Betta fish are some of the brightest fish in the sea! Take a look at these pictures, then finish off your own Betta fish using your own design.

Male Betta fish blow bubbles to create foamy nests to keep their young safe.

BRAIN-BUSTING BLUE WHALES!

Read these questions all about the incredible blue whale,
then see if you can find the correct answer on the list.

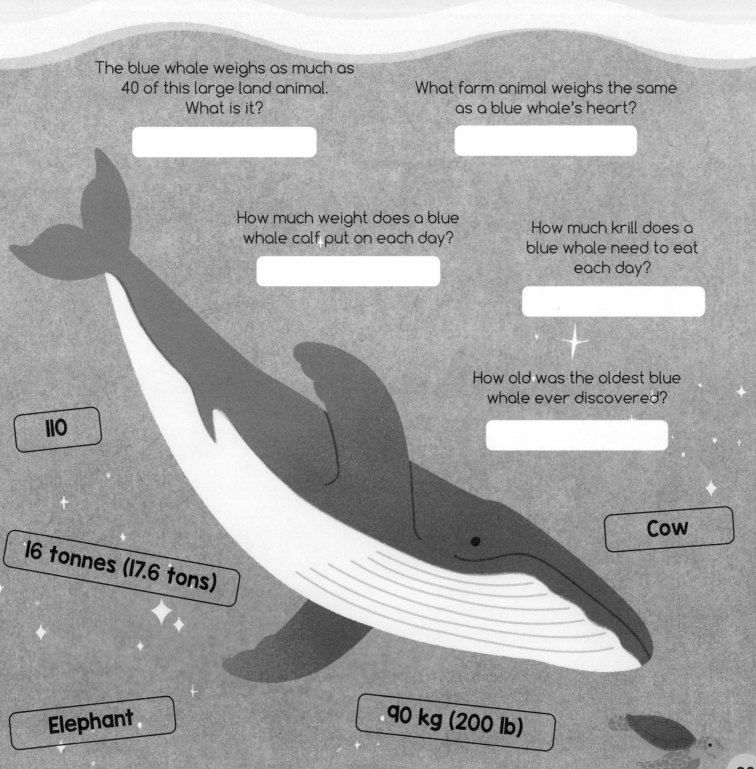

The blue whale weighs as much as
40 of this large land animal.
What is it?

What farm animal weighs the same
as a blue whale's heart?

How much weight does a blue
whale calf put on each day?

How much krill does a
blue whale need to eat
each day?

How old was the oldest blue
whale ever discovered?

110

16 tonnes (17.6 tons)

Cow

Elephant

90 kg (200 lb)

TEST YOUR OCEAN KNOWLEDGE!

So, how much have you learned about the world's ocean life? See how many questions you can answer (you can flip back through the book to find the answers!).

1. In which animal do clownfish live?

2. What type of ball is roughly the same size as the Pearl of Puerto—the world's largest pearl?

3. How long do stingrays live for?

4. What's the top speed at which a great white shark can swim?

5. Which type of whale makes the loudest sound of any animal on Earth?

6. How many eggs does a lionfish produce each year?

7. What type of ball is around the same size as a giant squid's eye?

8. What is the "fairy penguin" also known as?

HOW CAN YOU HELP THE OCEANS?

It's really important that we all do our bit to protect the oceans.
Here's how you can help at home!

Recycle or reuse your plastic

Plastic harms millions of marine animals every year, whether it's getting stuck inside plastic bottles or eating small bits of plastic. Make sure to recycle as much plastic as you can by asking a grown-up how your local recycling system works. Carry a reusable water bottle with you instead of buying water.

Reduce your water use

Using less water helps to reduce your carbon footprint (the amount of energy you use up). Try not to leave the water running while you brush your teeth, and take showers more often than baths.

Beach clean-up!

If you live near a beach, chances are that there will be a regular organized clean-up to get involved with. If you can't find one, why not ask a grown-up to help you set one up? Even if you only visit a beach now and then, you can help out by collecting any litter you see and recycling it or throwing it away (don't forget to wash or sanitize your hands afterward).

ANSWERS

Page 4
Under the sand.

Page 5

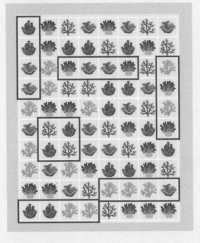

Page 6

Page 8

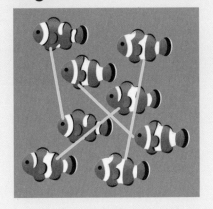

Page 9

Pages 10-11

Page 12
These statements are false:
* The trench is named after the diver who discovered it. **It is actually named after the Mariana Islands, which are nearby.**
* The last species to be discovered in the trench was in 1981. **It was actually in 2017 and was a type of snailfish.**
* It is impossible for a human to reach the bottom. **The first people to reach the bottom did it in 1960.**

Page 13

Hammerhead shark to squid.
Green sea turtle to algae.
Octopus to sea snail.
Blue whale to krill.

Page 14

You pass seven fish.

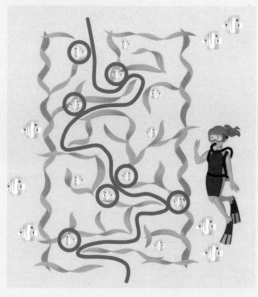

Page 15

The missing pieces are A, B, and F.

Pages 16-17

Anglerfish: 2
Viperfish: 1
Rattails: 3
Football fish: 2
Blue tangs: 9

Page 18

* How long does the average walrus live?
  40 years
* How far away can a walrus' song be heard?
  16 km (10 miles)
* How long is the average walrus' tusk?
  100 cm (40 in)
* Which part of its body does a walrus use to hunt and to pull itself out of the water?
  Tusks
* How much can a male walrus weigh?
  2 tonnes (2.2 tons)

Page 19

1. Four. If you are sharing the cake with three other people, then one slice must be for you!
2. Five
3. Three
4. Two

Page 20

E.

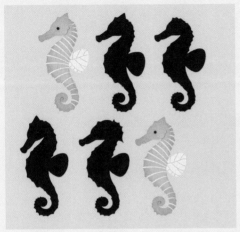

Page 21

It is a turtle.

Page 22

 Blue whale

 Beluga whale

 Sperm whale

 Humpback whale

Page 23

Herbivores
* Green sea turtle
Omnivores
* Angelfish
* Saltwater crab
* Bonnethead shark
Carnivores
* Tuna
* Orca
* Great white shark
* Walrus
* Porpoise

Page 26

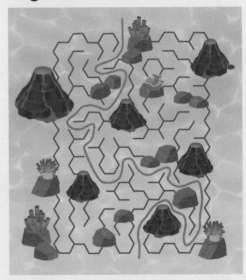

Page 27

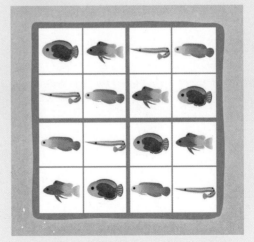

Pages 28–29

Page 31

These statements are false:

* Great white sharks chew up their food.
  They rip their prey into chunks and swallow
  these whole.
* They grow to 2 m (6.5 ft) long. They can
  actually grow to 6 m (19.6 ft) long!

Pages 32–33

Page 34

Page 35

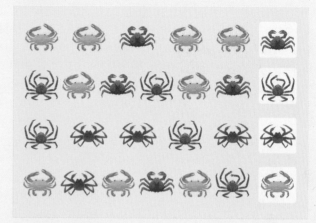

Pages 36–37

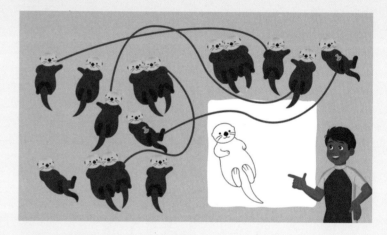

Page 38

The missing pieces are B, C, and E.

Page 39

 Thorny seahorse

 Weedy seadragon

 Leafy seahorse

 Pygmy seadragon

Page 40

* How many Atlantic bluefin tuna can be found in a school? **45**
* How long can the Atlantic bluefin tuna grow? **3 m (10 ft)**
* How heavy was the biggest tuna ever caught? **678 kg (1,496 lb)**
* How deep can a southern bluefin tuna dive in a day? **1,000 m (3,280 ft)**
* How fast can yellowfin tuna swim? **74 km/h (46 mph)**

Page 41

Pages 42–43

The seal is at grid reference J11.

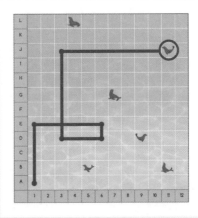

Page 44

 Sea urchin = 5

 Starfish = 3

 Stickleback = 6

 Shrimp = 10

Page 45

E, D, B, F, C, A.

Page 46

The missing pieces are A, D, and F.

Page 47

There are 22 plastic bottles.

Page 48

It is a lobster.

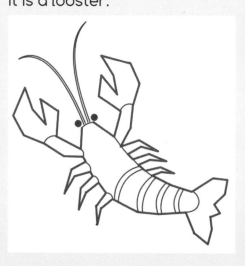

Page 49

The odd one out is C. The middle part is thicker than it is in the others.

Pages 50–51

Page 52

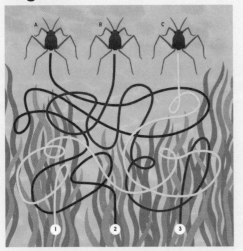

Page 53

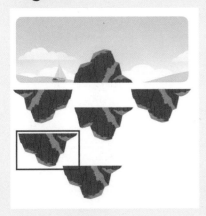

Page 54

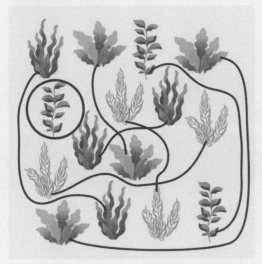

Page 55

The missing pieces are B, C, and F.

Page 56

It is the Burmeister's porpoise.

Page 57

Scallop shell = 3

Cowrie shell = 9

Nautilus shell = 6

Sand dollar shell = 7

Pages 58–59

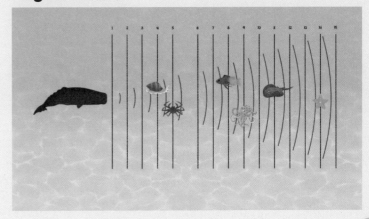

Page 60

Page 61

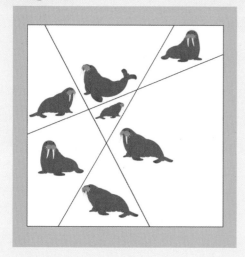

Page 62

There are 13 plankton.

Page 64

1. They are mostly awake during the night.
2. They have venomous spines along their backs.
3. They are carnivores and eat over 50 different types of other fish.
4. They can each produce 2 million eggs in a year.

Page 65

These statements are false:
* They only eat plants and algae. **They are actually carnivores.**
* They have only been found in the Atlantic Ocean. **Giant squid remains have been found in every ocean.**

Page 66

Venomous
* Box jellyfish
* Blue-ringed octopus
* Marbled cone snail

Non-venomous
* Horseshoe crab
* Dugong
* Tiger shark

Pages 67–68

1. Seven
2. Yes
3. No
4. Dolphin
5. Picture 3
6. Two

Page 69

Here is one possible answer:

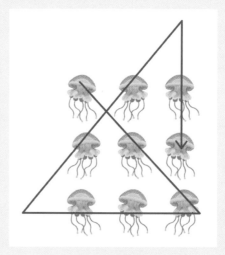

Page 70

$0.5 + 0.5 = 1$

$15 \div 5 = 3$

$48 \div 12 = 4$

$30 - 25 = 5$

$36 \div 6 = 6$

Page 71

Lemon shark

Megamouth shark

Cookie cutter shark

Nurse shark

Pages 72–73

Starfish: 11
Lobsters: 3
Pink coral: 7
Blue tangs: 12
Anchors: 1

Page 74

Atlantic spotted dolphin

Bottlenose dolphin

Dusky dolphin

Spinner dolphin

Page 75

Page 76

The submarine is heading to square G2.

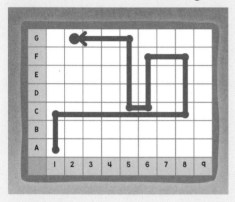

Page 77

Pages 78–79

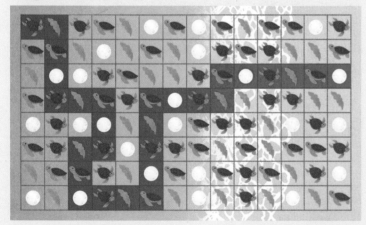

Page 80

* These penguins have bright orange on their beaks. Their chicks have large, shaggy feathers that make them look bigger than their parents! **King penguin**
* This type is sometimes called the "fairy penguin" because of its small size! **Australia little penguin**
* These don't slide on their bellies like most penguins. Instead, they prefer to hop about on land. **Rockhopper penguin**
* These penguins prefer a warmer place to nest and have white markings around their eyes. **Galápagos penguin**

Page 81

Zebra seahorse: 9
Long-snouted seahorse: 7
Lined seahorse: 8

Page 83

* The blue whale weighs as much as 40 of this large land animal. What is it? **Elephant**
* What farm animal weighs the same as a blue whale's heart? **Cow**
* How much weight does a blue whale calf put on each day? **90 kg (200 lb)**
* How much krill does a blue whale need to eat each day? **16 tonnes (17.6 tons)**
* How old was the oldest blue whale ever discovered? **110**

Pages 84–85

1. In anemones
2. Soccer ball
3. Up to 25 years
4. 56 km/h (35 mph)
5. Sperm whale
6. 2 million
7. Basketball
8. Australia little penguin